Bullying

Managing fear in young children

by
Dr Hannah Mortimer
and
Alan Johnson

and illustrated by Robyn Gallow

Acknowledgement
With acknowledgements and thanks to Jackie Johnson.
Many thanks to Chris Grimsley and Glenda Sutcliffe of The Instit2ute of NLP for Public Service for their ongoing support and inspiration for using NLP to help people who work with people, and for their helpful NLP training notes.

A QEd Publication

Published in 2009

ISBN 978 1 898873 60 0

British Library Cataloguing
A catalogue record for this book is available from the British Library.

Published by QEd Publications, 39 Weeping Cross, Stafford ST17 0DG
Tel: 01785 620364
Fax: 01785 607797
Web site: www.qed.uk.com
Email: orders@qed.uk.com

Printed by Gutenberg Press, Malta.

Contents

Introduction

Who the book is for

This book is part of a series written to help adults provide emotional support to young children aged 5 to 11. Sometimes teasing and bullying get in the way of their happiness, well-being and self-development. This book focuses on building children's self-esteem, helping them to develop emotional resilience and helping them to spot 'when their buttons are being pressed' by others who do not have their best interests at heart. There are similar books in the series on managing anxiety (*Worry Box*) and anger management (*Fireworks*). The books are written in an accessible and practical style so that a parent, carer, support assistant, childminder or mentor can work out the most suitable approach for the individual child concerned and 'pick and mix' activities and talking points to fill a number of sessions.

Why was this book written?

These books were written to fill a perceived need. When a child is suffering because of persistent teasing or where a child has been bullied, the adults in their lives are often left feeling 'if only I could do something to help . . .'. In the authors' experience, there are several very useful books available for dealing with bullying in schools (some of these are listed on pages 52 and 53), but fewer available for working with individual children age four to eleven who have been bullied. One of the authors found herself adapting material to suit these younger children and writing individual packages so that parents or professionals could support the children they were working with. This book provides one approach using powerful techniques taken from NLP (Neuro-linguistic Programming).

The approach is just one piece of wider work to investigate the problem of bullying and manage it within a social context. Where professionals and parents are concerned that a child is particularly vulnerable to teasing and is being upset and unsettled by this, and it is evident that this acts as a barrier to the child's happiness or well-being, they sometimes want a discreet approach for helping the child to cope better. The approach in this book aims to provide a practical framework for you to 'get started'.

The talk-through approach described in this book should never be seen as the sole solution in a case of bullying and all schools should have policies and procedures which enable them to look into and deal with bullying appropriately. It may not be helpful to see bullying behaviour in terms of a 'bullier' and 'victim'; neither would it be helpful to try to address the problem by working with just one or the other. Bullying takes place in a social context – hence the need for whole-school approaches.

The terminology used in this book refers to children being 'teased or bullied' so as not to lose time in having to distinguish between the two. This is an approach based on empowerment of the individual child. For some children, persistent teasing is as damaging as outright bullying, especially if they do not yet have the skills to understand or cope with it.

Of course, if you offer this approach and the child is just as vulnerable or affected at the end of the course, you are advised to seek further professional support. You would also stop the course and seek advice if it was making the child much more anxious than before. You should always talk to the school if that is where the bullying is taking place. If the child has been following the approach at school, then a referral from the SENCO (Special Educational Needs Coordinator) to a behaviour support teacher or worker, or educational psychologist would be an option. Please share what you are doing between home and school so that the work can be carried out within the context of the wider anti-bullying framework.

'Talk through' approaches

The books use a 'talk through' approach to provide a framework for the adult and child to talk and work together. You might have met this approach before in the other books in this series. The words in the framework are a guide and work best when used flexibly for the individual child, so that each piece of work seems to flow naturally and feel appropriate for your situation. You are encouraged to think creatively as you work together with the child and to adapt or even design your own sessions as they develop. Though much of it is written as an interaction between an adult and child, it is up to the adult to phrase the wording, and adapt it to suit the situation, age and stage of the child.

What do we know about emotions?

Emotions are the names we give to recognisable sets of feelings, sensations and thoughts; these in turn decide our behaviour. Our thoughts, feelings and behaviour are inter-dependent and linked, so changing one can change the other two. We will be describing easy ways for children to do this, so they can think, feel and behave differently in a positive and helpful way.

We know that anxiety and reactions to stress are controlled within the brain and the nervous system. We know that it originates in the 'fight or flight' mechanism we needed for survival as cave dwellers. It was important for us to have a rapid mechanism that allowed us to see a beast and make a split-second decision as to whether to chase and attack it or whether to flee for our lives. It was no good pausing to think about it. This is why the emotional part of our brain is sometimes called the 'primitive' area of the brain – it acts without logical thought and almost despite ourselves.

Nowadays, even though we may have evolved and developed much higher thinking skills, our emotional brains continue to be vitally important for learning which things in life to avoid and which to approach and explore. Very young children are inevitably driven more by their emotional brains than their logic – they are 'all needs and reactions'. However, in time, toddlers and pre-school children develop the language and understanding needed to link their emotional feelings to their words and their experiences and thereby to develop 'emotional literacy'.

The fact is that our emotional brains can switch in without us being fully aware of why or where the feelings are coming from. Some people talk about this phenomenon as forming part of our 'emotional intelligence' – if we can understand where our feelings are coming from and what emotional experiences or 'baggage' have formed them, then we are emotionally intelligent individuals. For many of us, the picture is complex and we have work to do on developing our 'emotional literacy' if we are to be better able to handle our emotions. Feeling teased or bullied adds to this 'baggage' significantly and children can feel their emotions triggered by events which, for most of us, might go without notice. In other words, they can become almost 'over-sensitive' to situations.

That, in a nutshell, is what this series is about – helping even young children to develop their emotional intelligence when it seems that their emotional brains continue to shout louder than their logical brains. Some children find it hard to integrate their emotions with their experiences and they remain very emotional individuals who *react* rather than *consider*.

The book is based loosely on cognitive behavioural therapy and Neuro-linguistic Programming (NLP) in which the child is helped to think about their feelings and behaviours in a different way and thereby to feel more in control of them and their resulting behaviours. You will also find some of the ideas from attachment theory and an approach called 'solution focused therapy'. These approaches are not magic wands and should never be used as a sticking plaster for serious emotional problems – 'fixing' a behaviour on the surface cannot also address an underlying emotional difficulty. That is why the approach is sometimes used as part of a wider menu of support with the aid of an outside professional. Nevertheless, if an emotional behaviour is getting in the way of a child's progress and happiness and if the child recognises this and wants to do some work on it, then it is well worth while trying the approach using the tools and techniques shown in this book within a home or educational setting.

This book will empower children prone to being bullied by other children by:

- identifying strategies to minimise the chances of being picked on;
- helping the child to cope when being teased or approached by children who bully;
- preventing future episodes of teasing or bullying by
  - empowering the child to feel differently about themselves, so they are less bothered by others' words or actions;
  - improving the child's presentation/behaviour around other children to be less attractive to children who bully;
  - giving the child strategies to think differently about the situation, so that their new way of thinking is more helpful to them than their current pattern of thinking.

How to use this book

Chapter One helps you to get started. You need to think about who will do the work and how to involve and engage the child fully in what you are doing. Chapter Two suggests twelve sessions that can be used flexibly and adapted to suit your situation, whether working at home with your own child or in an educational or out-of-school setting. In Chapter Three, there is some general information about bullying, including anti-bullying policies. At the end of the book is a Resources section with helpful books, resources and a list of useful organisations.

Throughout the book there are boxed guidance sections for the adult. There are also activity sheets and questionnaires to enlarge and photocopy or draw your own version of. These are for the child to complete with your help and to stick into their work file or scrapbook.

Chapter 1

Getting Started

Involve the child

First of all, you need to identify that there is a problem. There is no point embarking on this work if the child sees no need or does not understand what it is about. Something brought you to the point where you obtained this book and considered doing some work with the child. Put this into words and write it down for yourself. For example: 'Josh has been bullied at his last school. I thought we had dealt with it but he still seems to be upset and he doesn't have many friends at his new school. I think it really affected his confidence and I just want him to be happier about school and friendships.'

So far, you have *your* reasons for working together, but they might not be Josh's. Look at what you have written and you might find one or two statements that are concrete, indisputable and clearly a problem for Josh. For example: 'You really want to make new friends. You had a bad time at your last school because some pupils were very unkind and you were bullied. This makes it harder for you to trust friends now. Shall we try to stop the bad memories getting in the way of making new friends?'

Who is the best person to help?

If you are following the approach at home and there is more than one possible adult helper, talk to the child about who they would like to do their work with. Accept your child's choice, even if your child chooses the other parent or another relative – usually each parent is best for meeting different needs in their child. Whichever of you is chosen, make this an absolute priority and keep regular, protected time for it. Make sure you also have enough time to clear your own mind and become calm and receptive before beginning each session.

If the approach is being used in school or another setting, then decide who will be regularly available for the child and whom the child already feels close to and can trust. This might be a personal support assistant or a teacher who has been released by a classroom support assistant. Some schools might have carefully selected and screened volunteer mentors or parent helpers. This kind of work is also possible to do in out-of-school settings where there is a small amount of training and ongoing support from, for example, a Children's Centre team or family support workers. Sometimes these kind of approaches are also used by community nurses or occupational therapists in Child and Adult Mental Health Services (CAMHS). The work should always have the full support and involvement of parents or carers.

A shopping list

You will need:

- an A4 box file, preferably new, 'cool' and one the child has chosen;
- a pack of brand new felt-tip pens in many colours;
- a craft box with scissors, glue stick, hole punch, thicker felt-tips etc.;
- a scrap book, A4 file pad or stack of A4 paper.

Put everything in the box file and keep it all safe and out of circulation between sessions.

A quiet corner

You also need to decide on a quiet place to be together for about 45 minutes each time for about ten to twelve sessions. Try to always work in the same 'secure base'. Because the whole course will take several sessions, it is best to find a slot in your week when you both know you can be together on your own – plan it rather like a music lesson. You might decide to work once a week. You might enjoy it so much that you choose twice a week. Don't rush it any faster than that because it needs time to 'cook' in the child's head between sessions!

Planning your sessions

Read the whole book first so that you, the adult, know broadly what you will be doing together. Plan the first two or three sessions carefully, and then let the course take its own direction as your work together proceeds. Keep the content of future sessions secret from the child so that each session comes as a good surprise. Explain to the child that a lot of the work you do will be fun, even though it also has its serious side. By the end of the course you will both have learned lots about how the child's emotional thinking works and how they can develop new strategies for when they are needed.

Ages and stages

Though the text tells the child to 'read' or 'write' something, you can adapt how you do the activities depending on the age and stage of the child. Younger children will need you to do a lot of the reading and writing, although even six year-olds can tell you what they want you to write for them or may want to copy pieces into their scrapbook if you help or draw pictures. Stay flexible and allow each session to run comfortably – even into the next, as you find some take longer or less time than others. Above all, 'go with the child' so that you are both really engaging with and thinking about your work together.

We wanted to use this approach because Junaid seemed to be such a loner at school. He often came home and told us he had been teased and we could never really sort out what was going on. We were confused about whether or not he was being bullied. Actually, when we started this work, he began to talk with us much more. It turned out that there was one boy at school who was making his life pretty miserable. We sorted out what to do about it and spoke to the school. Junaid also found he didn't become so worked up and he stopped letting this other lad get the better of him.

Father of Junaid, aged 9

Chapter 2

Twelve practical sessions

These sessions are written as an interaction between an adult and child. This avoids specifying gender and also makes the text seem more personal and directly relevant. For very young children, you will need to do all the reading, of course, and adapt the words to suit a younger age. For all children, you need to interpret the text flexibly and alter the style to suit your situation. The words simply give you both a starting point for the work you are doing together.

The sessions are numbered, but should not be followed blindly. After the first three sessions, adjust and develop as the child and the situation begin to lead you. The very first session is deliberately more impersonal than the rest to give you both time to settle in. You will also find boxed sections of further information for the adult helper.

If you are working as a professional, make it clear that your work is confidential unless you have any concerns about keeping the child safe or breaking the law. Safeguarding Children (Child Protection) procedures are paramount over everything else you do in this course.

Session 1	Making a work box

Hello . . . . . Well done – it is great that you have decided to do something to help you feel happier and find it easier to make friends again. This will be enjoyable and useful. Is there anything you would like to ask before we get started?

The first thing to do is to prepare your work box. This is your new box file. Decorate a large label and stick it onto the front – and name it 'MY WORK BOX – STRICTLY SECRET' and have your name on in large decorated letters. Once you have decorated your work box, we'll make sure we can be together so that you can share it with me and I can admire it.

Well done . . . . . that's the end of your first session! Where do you think I can put your work box so we can keep it somewhere safe?

Notes for adults

Keep this work personal by using the child's name frequently. Try to let the child work as independently as possible on their work box so that they feel proud of what they have done and personally involved with the work you will be doing together. Use this session to settle in together and keep it relaxed and encouraging.

Notes for adults

We can often assume we know what we, or someone close to us, really wants. How can we be sure we've got it right? The technique below known as POSSEE ensures that any goal or outcome is stated positively and is planned in a well-rounded way. This ensures the outcome is real, achievable and motivates the person towards it.

Use the activity worksheet on pages 16 and 17 to discuss what the child would like to have happen about the problem of bullying.

This is written in adult language – please take the principles and adapt them for your child's understanding and learning style. There are examples to guide you. Try and avoid putting words into their mouths.

Here are the rules for how to write a *well formed outcome.* Use these as a guide to completing the worksheet.

P POSITIVE

Help the child state this in terms of what they want, rather than a 'don't want'. We are all very good at identifying what we don't want, rather than what we do want to have happen. If you stop to think about it, this is rather like going shopping at the supermarket with a list of the 10,000 things we don't need rather than the 100 we do – very difficult to achieve!

Example: If a child states 'I don't want to be bullied any more', ask 'What would you like instead?'

O OWN PART

Help the child acknowledge their own part in achieving the outcome. People, whether children or adults, can often blame other people or things for their current problems. Although others may have an influence or impact on the problem, the only person you can truly change is yourself, so you must take responsibility and ownership to remedy your problems. So ask the child, 'What will you do? How can you start and maintain it?'

Example: 'I will tell the appropriate adult as soon as I feel threatened.'

S SPECIFIC

If we make vague statements about what we want, we may get a vague result. Being very specific and accurate about what we want makes it more real and more easily achieved. So encourage the child to think about:

- **What** do I want, what will I be doing?
- **When** will I be doing it, when will I know?
- **Where** will I be doing it (perhaps the most challenging place)?
- **How** will I be doing it (easily, happily . . .)?
- **With whom**, if anybody specifically?

Example: 'I would like to be happy at school, free to play as I like with three friends. I will be doing this every day and it will be very easy for me to do this.'

S SIZE

We need to be sure that what we want is of an achievable size. If we need to break it down to a few goals in several stages, this may be more useful. So help the child think about:

- Is the outcome the right size? If it is too large, break it down into smaller outcomes that are clear and achievable.

Example: 'To achieve the goal I have described above I will start by playing with one close friend.'

E EVIDENCE

Using language specific to the senses in order to help the child to see, hear and feel the way it will be *when* they have got what they want. It is not a matter of *if*, only *when* it will happen. Encourage the child to think about:

- **How** will you know when you've achieved your outcome?
- **What** will you see, feel, and hear? (Encourage the child to see it through their own eyes, rather than you, the adult, being in the scene too).

Example: 'I will see friendly and happy faces, hear people calling my name as friends, and I will feel happy and confident. I will know this as I will feel warm in my tummy.'

E ECOLOGY

By ecology, we mean how would any changes you can make affect other people – family, school friends, teachers, etc. Sometimes when we change, other people need to catch up to believe that we genuinely are different now ('If I change, everyone around me *has* to change'). Check out the consequences of the outcome. Ask the child: 'If you could have it now, would you take it? How might achieving the outcome affect other aspects of your life, or other people?'

Example: 'When I feel this confidence and happiness, people will be less able to bully me. My friends will like the changes in me, and my family will be very happy for me. School will have fewer problems to deal with.'

Activity sheet – knowing what I want

P POSITIVE
What do you want (stated *positively*)?

I want ....

....

....

O OWN PART
What is your (own) part? What will you do to start and keep things going to get this?

I will ....

....

S SPECIFIC
Specifically when, what, where, how and with whom do you want it?

I want ....

....

....

....

S SIZE
Is this something you know you can get?

....

....

Activity sheet – knowing what I want

E   EVIDENCE

How will you know when you have achieved your outcome? What will you see, hear and feel? What is the evidence?

When I have ...., I will

see ....

hear ....

feel ....

E   ECOLOGY

What things will happen when you have ....? How will it be?

The consequences for me are ....

....

The consequences for others are ....

....

When someone likes to bully others, they usually know who to pick on instinctively. Often it is the very subtle, unconscious signals that are picked up by the bully's radar which says: 'they will allow me to bully them'. Let's look at a first technique to make you less attractive to any bullies you meet.

Notes for adults

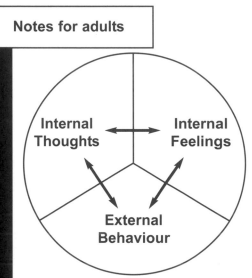

In NLP internal thoughts, internal feelings and external behaviour are all interlinked and affect each other. Changing one changes them all.

To change thoughts or feelings we may use various types of talking approaches. Sometimes these processes can be lengthy or people may feel inhibited to address these factors.

The quickest and easiest way is to shift *behaviour* – and this has instantaneous results in changing feelings and thoughts. Also, it can be done at almost any time or in any place.

In this case when we are talking about *external* behaviour, we mean body posture, gestures, eye movements, what we say etc.

Why work on this?

There is a phenomenon known as 'victim posture' – eyes down, shoulders and chest slumped over, tentative movement, deep sighing, unsteady voice and so on. It has been noted that people who present in this way

- don't *feel* too good, and
- create a 'self-fulfilling prophecy' so that other people see and treat them as victims.

When people are experiencing unhelpful, depressing or de-motivating *thoughts* or *feelings*, they tend to adopt some or all of this *behaviour*, which can lead to a downward spiral into unhelpful thoughts or feelings.

Standing Firm: 'I'm no Push-over!'

Evidence of imbalance

Get the child to stand with their arms by their sides, feet slightly apart and eyes closed. Gently push one shoulder, being ready to steady them safely, just to demonstrate how unbalanced physically they probably are. This is because most people concentrate their attention on their head, causing them to be off-balance and easy to push over. To help the child from being an easy 'push-over', follow the steps below (taken partly from the martial art, Aikido).

'Put your brain in your tummy'

Hold your hand in front of the child's head/face (where their centre of focus currently is) and ask them to shift their focus of attention to your hand. Without touching, slowly move your hand down to the area in front of their navel, and just below – ask them to follow it with their attention, placing their 'brain in their tummy'.

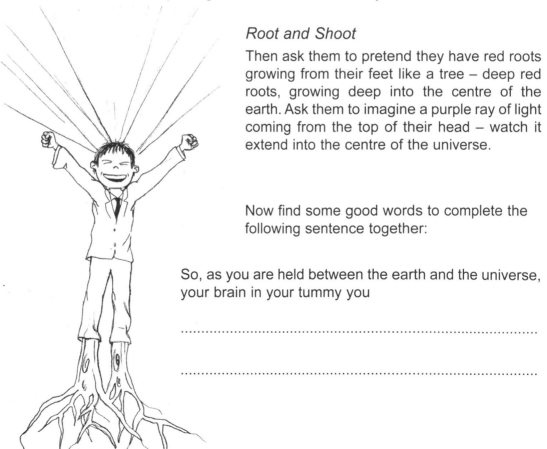

Root and Shoot

Then ask them to pretend they have red roots growing from their feet like a tree – deep red roots, growing deep into the centre of the earth. Ask them to imagine a purple ray of light coming from the top of their head – watch it extend into the centre of the universe.

Now find some good words to complete the following sentence together:

So, as you are held between the earth and the universe, your brain in your tummy you

....

....

To connect the sentence or 'saying' to a sound, get the child to choose a word or phrase to say out loud, such as 'Stand firm!' or something else empowering as a signal to return to this state.

Test the change

While they hold this state, once again push them gently as before – they will be solid and should not move. Repeat the process, if necessary, to make it even stronger and more empowering. The child can recall this phrase whenever they need to feel strong and grounded. It will also help them if they are being physically jostled.

Walking Tall: thinking about posture

Encourage the child to improve their posture and attitude about themselves by coaching them to:

- sit or stand up really tall and straight;
- set their shoulders back and chest out;
- breathe regularly, rhythmically and intentionally;
- look up (away from those negative feelings – we look down when we are sad);
- walk with purpose.

Experiment by walking around the room, head down and shoulders slumped. How does it feel? Now try holding your head up, shoulders back and smiling. How does it feel *now*?

Having mastered the steps above, ask them if it is possible to have bad, negative or unhelpful thoughts and notice the difference!

<table>
<tr><td>Session 4</td><td># Making it less likely that you will be bullied</td></tr>
</table>

Self-esteem

Work on keeping your self-esteem high. Tell yourself that you're 'worth it' and think positively about all the things that make you likeable and loved.

Write down all of the people who think you are special	
Why do you think they like you so much?	

Understanding bullying

Make sure you talk to someone. This is *very* important because bullying is *always* wrong. There are different types of bullying. The thing is – if you *feel* bullied you *are* being bullied. Hurting your feelings over and over again is called 'emotional bullying' and this is wrong too.

Write down the different types of bullying you can think of?	
Who would you talk to if you were being bullied?	
Why do you think the bully is behaving that way?	

Some tips

- Aim to make plenty of friends and go around in a group.
- Avoid situations where you could be singled out and hurt.

What to do if you are actually being bullied

1) If you know the person, try making it personal by using the bully's name and looking the bully straight in the eye (without being threatening). This might make the bully remember that you are both people and ought to treat each other with respect.

2) If some of your friends were watching and seemed to be joining in, speak to them later one by one and let them know how it made you feel.

3) Use a new approach – smile and be nice to them – it's easier to bully someone who looks scared than someone who is being nice to you!

4) Tell them what will happen if they carry on. In other words, warn them that there would be consequences (for example: 'if you do that again I will have to tell [the teacher]'). Keep repeating this like a 'broken record' and ignore it if they continue to try to wind you up. Do what you say if the bully doesn't stop.

5) Run if they are going to start trying to hurt you. Get yourself somewhere safe – to a teacher, your home or a public place.

6) Practise what you might say to a bully with someone you like to talk to.

Think through these suggestions and write a plan for some of the things you will do to make you stronger and safer against bullies.

My plan of action

Session 5	Magic fingers
	Giving children resources to use in any situation

Notes for adults

Giving a child access to any 'resource' at will, can be very empowering. Resources here refers to attributes such as 'strength', 'courage' and 'happiness'. These resources can be 'placed' on a child's fingers, knuckles or by making a fist, for instance.

This works on the principle of 'anchoring' – a simple form of conditioning that we all respond to . . . it makes our familiar sofa seem even more comfortable; it makes a certain song remind us of something in the past; it may link a feeling or memory to a specific part of the body.

In this session you are going to help the child re-live an event that has a powerful attribute (such as 'courage') to use as a resource. Find a quiet time and space and follow the instructions below. Keep in mind the positive philosophy that we have all the internal resources we need or can create them.

Practical strategies

1) Talk to the child and discover a resource/feeling that they would find useful in a specific situation in the future. For example, they may want to *feel strong* when walking past another child.

2) Agree a physical gesture that will become the anchor or 'magic fingers' – touching a knuckle, placing two fingers together, clenching a fist etc.

3) Get the child to remember a specific time that they experienced that feeling 'strong' (for example, a sports achievement). Be sure to choose a vivid and *powerful* example. If the child does not have an example of their own, get them to imagine how it would be for someone they know, someone from TV, a film or a comic book hero. If it is imagined vividly enough it will still work.

4) Ask the child to close their eyes and remember or imagine that experience and feeling of 'strong' in vivid detail.

5) Guide them to re-live it in full detail and intensity through their own eyes (even if pretending). What do they *see*, *hear* and *feel*? You can do this by encouraging them to:
   – make the picture lighter or the colours brighter;
   – bring the image closer;
   – make the sounds clearer or louder;
   – link it to a word that makes the feeling even better such as 'strong', 'great!', 'yahoo!'.

6) As this feeling begins to grow, you need to help the child create a strong association between this feeling and the physical gesture they have chosen (e.g. touching a knuckle, placing two fingers together, clenching a fist). You do this by applying the 'anchor' the child has chosen – for example, making a fist.

7) When the feeling is reaching its peak of intensity, release the 'anchor'. The diagram below will help you as you observe the child's reaction in order to judge the intensity of the visualised experience.

8) Get the child to open his/her eyes, and distract them by asking them an irrelevant question, or getting them to spin around, count to 10 etc. This is called 'breaking state'.

9) Repeat the above several times (minimum of five), each time guiding them to increase the vivid nature of the experience by making increases in picture and sound quality and intensity of feelings. Each time break state in between.

10) Test the anchor is working by 'firing' it (press the knuckle, put fingers together). Ask the child what happens. After going through the strategy, the child will begin to experience strength from within, purely by firing the anchor.

11) Get the child to think about a situation in the future when they may need strength (walking past a particular child perhaps). Run the scene, getting the child to fire their anchor at the time they need 'strength' and notice how it *feels* different.

12) Add more resources (e.g. courage, happiness) to the same or other knuckles or other gestures as required.

13) Check the anchor the following day and get the child to keep firing it to make it permanent.

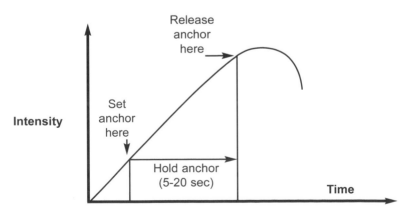

24

Session 6	**Getting support**

Our fears tend to shrink when we have lots of support. You have your family, your home and also your friends, and now you have your 'Magic fingers'. When you know what things support you, you can actually plan extra support when you need it.

In this session we're going to talk about friends and write down your thoughts.

What do you think a really good friend should be like?	
What would they do for you that was friendly?	
What would you do together?	
What would you talk about?	
What would your friend be like?	

This will help you to draw your own list of friends and helpers below. In the middle heart (nearest and dearest), put all the people who will support you whatever happens (like your family and close friends) – in the outer heart add the others who are also there for you (like teachers, other friends, doctor, etc).

The rest of this session is for making illustrations of your own friends and family and we will write a little about each of them for your work box. How does each one help to make you happy or stop you being afraid? What fears or worries would you talk to Mum/Dad/Nan about? What fears or worries would you talk to your friends about? What fears or worries would you talk to your teacher about?

Good luck! Make sure all your work sheets, pictures and pieces of writing are safely in your work box – it must be getting quite full now!

Session 7 — Getting things into proportion

NLP techniques demonstrate how we react to the 'movies' we make in our heads rather than the actual events we experience. This is why:

- dreams or nightmares feel so real;
- we can create anchors (magic fingers, Session 5) to feel recreated experiences;
- the same stimulus (e.g. a parachute jump) can make some people feel fear/anxiety and others feel excitement/buzz.

It is the representation in our head (pictures/sounds/self-talk) and body (feelings/sensations) that let us decide the meaning (naming an emotion – actioning a behaviour).

We tend to grade or sort things as good or bad, helpful or unhelpful, fearful or exciting. We will usually have one set of qualities for things we like and another for those we don't like so much. For example, think about your favourite food, then a food you would not eat. The representations in your head and body will probably be very different.

We can apply these phenomena to things like bullying and fear.

Sit down with the child and ask them to imagine an example of a scene where someone has teased or bullied them. It will be easier if they close their eyes and notice the pictures, sounds, self talk in their head to represent this and the feelings inside this creates. Using the framework below, ask for more details/qualities of the pictures/sounds and self-talk. Then explain to the child that you will be asking some unusual questions about colour and shape to give the feeling in their body an 'entity', something with visual and sound qualities. This may seem strange at first, but doing this gives us something tangible to work with rather than a vague, intangible 'feeling'.

If you find that the child finds it difficult at first, for example, if they say they don't know what colour the feeling is, just try prompts such as: 'and if you *did* know, what colour would it be?' or 'guess what colour it would be'. Even a guess comes from the subconscious representation of the feeling, so it must be 'right'.

Write down the word or phrase that describes your negative emotion (like 'feeling scared'). Give it a score of 0-10 to show the strength of it.	
Describe the qualities of the pictures and sounds you use in your head to represent the feeling.	
Describe the feeling: Where in your body is the feeling? What colour is it? What shape is it? What size, temperature etc?	
Now change the qualities of the pictures/sounds/feelings one at a time, using this phrase: "Notice what happens when you change the . . . through your own eyes. Does the feeling get better, worse or stay the same?"	

Make a note of any changes that significantly decrease the negative emotion, so that these can be highlighted.

It may be helpful when changing an unhelpful internal voice (such as the scary voice of a bully) into Mickey Mouse/Donald Duck rather than attempting to change the content – this makes it impossible to take seriously, and reduces the impact.

A detailed worksheet is provided on the following two pages to help in this exercise.

Getting things in proportion		
Quality	**Child's description**	**Changing things** If you change one thing, does your feeling get better, worse or stay the same?
Describe the qualities of the pictures and sounds you use in your head to represent the feeling Is it through your own eyes that you picture this . . . or do you see yourself in the picture?		
Does the picture have an edge to it (like a border)?		
Is the picture black and white or in colour?		
Is it bright or dim?		
Is it near to you or far away?		
Is it large or small?		
Is it like a photo or like a movie?		
Are things in the picture happening slowly, quickly or not moving at all?		
Describe the external sounds Is it loud or quiet?		
What are the voices like?		

Getting things in proportion (continued)		
Quality	**Child's description**	**Changing things** If you change one thing, does your feeling get better, worse or stay the same?
Describe the internal sounds Are you saying things to yourself?		
Is your voice loud or soft?		
Is your tone of voice helpful?		
Are the things you are saying to yourself helpful?		
Describe the feelings and sensations Where in your body is the feeling?		
Is the feeling large or small?		
What colour is the feeling?		
Is it heavy or light?		
Is the feeling strong or weak?		
Is it there constantly or only sometimes?		
Does the feeling have a texture (is it rough or smooth)?		
Does the feeling feel hot or cold?		
Does the feeling move (fast, slow)?		
What sound does the feeling make?		

Session 8 — Speaking out

Notes for adults

This session looks at how we often bottle up emotions rather than dealing with events. There are examples of how you can help the child recognise that there are different ways of dealing with stressful situations and that being assertive is something that can be learned.

Start by explaining that bad stress is stress which cannot go anywhere because it does not lead to action and we bottle it up instead. When we do this, the stress can come out again in all the wrong ways, at the wrong times and in the wrong places. Sometimes we bottle things up because we avoid saying what we feel when we need to. Therefore, you may need to do some work together on 'being assertive'. Talk about what this means. Should you always say what is on your mind? When is it best to 'bottle up'? For example, if your grandma gave you a present and you didn't like it, would you tell her? Think of some more examples and write them down together.

Talk about how people react differently when they feel stressed:

- some people speak out – this is being *assertive*
- some are *passive* – they do and say nothing and just let other people 'walk all over them' or just 'switch off'
- others get angry and 'stroppy'.

Try and encourage the child to think of specific examples of each of these reactions in the people he/she knows.

Use puppets or action characters to act out a few situations and show what a difference it makes. Here is an example you could try with two characters, Gib and Gub.

Gib starts to bully Gub (act this out with your characters)	
Gub's reaction	**What do you think happens?** (Talk about each)
Gub says and does nothing.	
Gub kicks up an enormous fuss and lashes out.	
Gub says, 'Please stop doing that. If you don't, I will have to tell the teacher'.	
Gub asks for help from a friend.	

Here are some ways you can learn to be more calm and assertive.

- Listening carefully to other people and respect their feelings.
- Not raising your voice in an angry way.
- Telling people how you are feeling.
- Asking nicely and calmly for things.
- Trying to work out how other people are feeling.
- Saying sorry when you know you've done something wrong.

Sometimes people can be very aggressive and this gets them into trouble. Does this apply to you ever?

- Shouting at people.
- Demanding things.
- Being rude and swearing at people when you don't get your way.
- Making others feel sad or uncomfortable.
- Hurting other people's feelings.
- Hitting out or kicking other people when they don't agree or want to play.

Use the activity sheet below to help you think about how you will aim to react to a situation.

My plan of action
I will aim to be more assertive when _____ happens.
I will do this by

Spend some time visualising this happening. How does it work? What does it feel like?

Now do it!

Learning to step back from unpleasant feelings

Notes for adults

It is very easy to return instantly to the 'victim posture' (see Session 3) once confronted by someone who wants to cause trouble with us and call us names. This can only happen if we allow it to, and we react by feeling all of the intended pain, creating unhelpful mindsets for ourselves like 'I must be unlovable', 'I'm stupid' or 'no one should like me'.

This section looks at helping the child to distance ('dissociate') themselves from the person being mean and calling them names, so that they feel it less personally than before. This can help them to form new, more helpful beliefs about themselves and what the other child's behaviour towards them means about them.

Being able to separate the *person* from their *behaviour* is empowering both from the perspective of understanding oneself ('I am not a victim or vulnerable – I am in control of me') and in understanding the other child ('s/he is not a bully – s/he *chooses* to be mean to me and others and I know the behaviour is about them and not me').

In this exercise, the aim is to help the child develop a strategy of dissociation.

We are going to learn a way to feel better in situations where someone is trying to upset or pick on you. This needs you to be able to imagine pictures in your head. Try it a few times until you can do it really well. After practising this, your brain will do it naturally and the problems will seem much easier to cope with.

The next time someone calls you a name or picks on you:

1) Imagine you (No. 2) are looking at yourself (No. 1) in the situation that you are in as if you were watching a DVD (this is called 'dissociation').

2) To keep this distance and safety, imagine a very thick sheet of glass (like in a sea life centre) between you and the things happening on the screen.

3) Step back from this again (this is called 'double dissociation'), so you (No.3) are watching yourself (No. 2), watching the movie of you (No. 1) through the thick glass.

Try it now. Imagine a time when someone picked on you. Run through the steps above and notice how much less the feelings bother you.

Now remember this as another tool in your toolkit to use when confronted by people.

Session 10   Thinking positively

Notes for adults

This session is easiest for children of about eight and over. Try adapting it for younger children if you think they can manage, or skip it until they are older.

Sometimes it is our *thinking* that gets us into trouble. Because we think fearful thoughts, we do fearful actions.

For example, imagine someone has pushed into you when you are playing outside. You have a choice how you think about this. You can either think: 'He wants to fight me' and start to feel frightened or you can think: 'He tripped' or 'He didn't mean it' or 'He's in a hurry' and just let him pass. *You don't have to react.*

In other words, it is our own fearful thoughts that trigger our feeling frightened. If you can spot that you tend to think like this, you can actually make yourself see things a new way and stop yourself being so fearful. This is another way of coping with bullies. Think of a few examples.

Example – someone in your class has snatched your bike from you.

Fearful thought: He wants trouble and he's going to get nasty if I object.

Fearful behaviour: Letting him get away with it.

Positive thought: He really likes my bike. I'm not surprised – it's a good one!

Positive behaviour: (Depending on your situation) Tell a teacher/wait for him to come back and tell him to ask nicely next time/try not to leave it unattended.

Now try and complete the following example.

Example – Someone waits for you after school, calls you names and tries to make you feel intimidated.

Fearful thought:

Fearful behaviour:

Positive thought:

Positive behaviour:

Your own example –

Fearful thought:

Fearful behaviour:

Positive thought:

Positive behaviour:

Let's talk about times when you have fearful thoughts. Think through times when people have made you really scared and then see whether there might have been another way to think about things. Sometimes, trying to put yourself in someone else's shoes is helpful – if you can work out why they appear to be intimidated themselves, it helps you explain why they are behaving like they are. This can help you not to get so fearful yourself.

I remember when . . . .

. . . .

made me really scared because . . . .

. . . .

I thought . . . .

. . . .

but perhaps I could have thought . . . .

. . . .

Session 11	# My Spotlight
	Stepping into a resourceful place at will

Notes for adults

This is a resource to empower children whenever they need to feel a positive emotion or state. Originally used in 'performance' situations such as public speaking, examinations, meetings and sport, this process can be used to increase a person's performance and resources in any situation. It uses a similar principle as anchoring in 'magic fingers' (Session 5), though it makes use of a 'spatial' anchor – an imaginary circle projected onto the floor.

This is another, very practical, tool to raise a child's esteem and confidence in any situation.

Assuming the desired resource you wanted to develop or increase is **confidence**:

1. Guide the child to relive the excellent state

In standing position, get them to go back to a specific time when they were very confident, *abundantly* confident – or pretend to be someone who has confidence (see Session 3). Guide them to relive that moment, seeing what they saw, hearing what they heard, and feeling the intensity of the experience.

2. Creating a spotlight

As the feeling builds, get them to imagine a coloured circle or ray of light on the floor around their feet. What colour is it? What about a sound that indicates how powerful it is? Let the feeling of confidence build and build, and as it does, let the spotlight grow and light envelop them. When the feeling of confidence is at its fullest, step out, leaving those confident feelings inside the spotlight.

3. Making the spotlight more powerful

Repeat the process several times, each time making the pictures, sounds and intensity of feelings even greater.

4. Select a reminder to access your spotlight

Guide the child to think of a specific time in the future when they want to have that feeling of confidence. See and hear what will be there just before wanting the feeling.

5. Linking

When they have those cues clear in their mind, get them to step back into the spotlight and feel those feelings of confidence again. Imagine the situation unfolding with these confident feelings fully available to the child.

6. Check results

Get the child to step out of the spotlight again, leaving the feelings behind. Ask them to think about the upcoming situation, and notice how the child feels about it now.

7. Build up the spotlight

The child can repeat the process, adding as many different resources – happiness, strength, calmness etc – each time enhancing the qualities of their spotlight.

<table>
<tr><td>**Session 12**</td><td>How did I do?</td></tr>
</table>

Congratulations on all the work you have done on your course. You now know a lot more about bullying, how you respond and how it affects you. You also have many tools and ways of coping and feeling better in any situation now.

In my tool box I now have these skills:

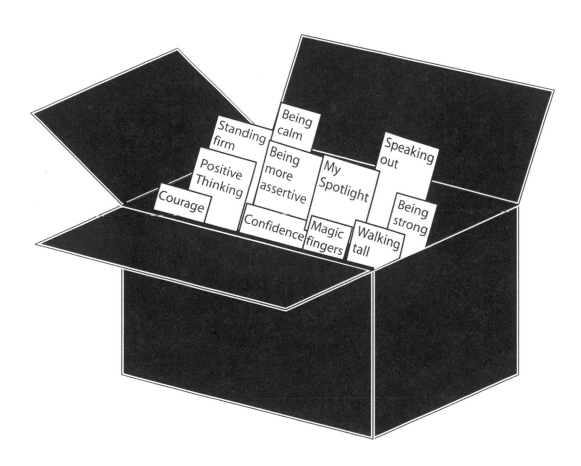

And now there's a special certificate for you.
CONGRATULATIONS! Plan a treat to celebrate.

I'm OK!

_____

has been working hard to manage their fears of bullying and has now come to the end of the course

Congratulations!

This is a REAL ACHIEVEMENT

Signed . . . .   Date . . . .

<table>
<tr><td>Chapter 3</td><td>

More about bullying

</td></tr>
</table>

In this chapter, you will read some general information for adults about bullying, its effects and how to plan an anti-bullying policy in your school or setting.

What is bullying?

When you ask young children what is meant by bullying, they come up with many answers.

Calling you names

looking at you to scare you

taking your stuff

hurting you

'dissing'

fighting

spreading rumours about you

saying lies about you

saying stuff about your family

saying things about your body

Hassling you when the teacher's not looking

racist remarks

General advice for parents and carers

It can be one of the most painful things you can do as a parent to watch your child suffer when you think they are being bullied. You might have noticed changes in their behaviour that were uncharacteristic or changes in their mood. They might not have told you that anything is wrong but you believe so nevertheless. You feel powerless and you long to help but know just how important it is not to make the situation worse for them.

Children don't always talk with their parents for many reasons. They might feel ashamed. They might feel scared that you will tell. They might even be angry with you all for not stopping it, without actually being able to put this into words. They might not want to worry you. Besides, 'telling tales' goes against all the rules of how to behave that you have amongst your friends. This is a lot for a young child to deal with – no wonder they are unhappy.

Bullying has to be tackled at adult level – your child is too young to be simply told to 'be more assertive'. Never tell them to be aggressive or violent back as this could have more serious repercussions and models how *not* to behave.

There are some key things to know and do:

- You need to remember that *bullying* is always wrong – *not* the child being subjected to the bullying.
- In the early stages, the important thing is to take what your child says seriously and believe them. Talk generally about bullying (this book will help) and help your child rehearse what they might do next time. Share with them ways of keeping safe – there are many suggestions in this book.
- Reassure your child that it is *not* your child's fault and stay calm so that you do not appear to be too anxious yourself.
- Contact the school since it is a disciplinary matter.
- The school should have an anti-bullying policy, so ask for a copy if you feel that the issue is not being taken seriously enough and persist with your concern. The teachers might not discuss fine detail with you (it would not be appropriate for them to share information with you about the other child) but should give you a clear indication of what they will do to address the problem and support your child.
- Ask the teachers to investigate and come back with you by a certain time, letting the Head or Deputy know what you have agreed.
- Keep a diary of incidents, what your child said, how your child was affected and anything you did to help.
- If you feel that you need further advice, you can contact the Anti Bullying Campaign or Parentline (see page 54). Your child should know that Childline can always be contacted for advice (page 54) and will involve the child all the way.

44

After you have shared all the events together, your child might feel quite traumatised and need close support and reassurance for a while afterwards. They might want to talk about what happened over and over – try to remain patient and encouraging. The other books in this series about managing anxiety and anger (see page 52) might be helpful for you if further work is required.

What does an anti-bullying policy look like?

All schools should have one and, as a parent, you can ask to see it. In fact, you *should* have a copy. The best policies usually contain this kind of information and there is more detailed and helpful information in the book and video resource *Safe to Tell* (see page 53).

Anti-Bullying Policy

1. The policy will usually start with a definition of bullying.
2. Next, it might describe how the school and parents will decide if an incident of bullying is 'serious'.
3. There should be a values statement about what the school sees to be important.
4. The policy would normally state who the policy is for – such as staff, pupils, parents and governors.
5. Sometimes there is a description of the extent of the problem.
6. A commitment to action: how children/teachers/parents will react when bullying takes place.
7. A plan for prevention describing a whole-school approach for dealing with bullying.
8. The strategy for awareness-raising might then be described.
9. There should be some indication of how the policy will be kept up to date.
10. Finally, the method of monitoring and evaluating the policy would normally be included.

Dealing with incidents in school

The two aims of any intervention in school should be:

- to make the bullied child feel safe;
- to encourage better behaviour from the child who has carried out the bullying, any colluders and observers.

The main approaches for dealing with bullying have tended to be to work with the bullied child in order to change their reaction in some way, to 'punish' the bullying child or to use a group problem-solving approach such as *The No Blame Approach* (Robinson and Maines, see page 53). This last approach helps both 'bully' and 'victim' (their terminology) to sort out the problem and encourages colluders and onlookers to take a more active stance in preventing bullying as well. After all, bullying takes place within a social context and, without the audience, much of the bully's power is defused.

In essence these steps are to talk with the victim, convene a meeting with the people involved, explain the problem, share responsibility for solving the problem, ask the group members for their ideas, leave it up to them and then meet them again for feedback (this is grossly over-simplified and you need to read the whole approach for the detail). In the author's experience, it has been a very helpful approach for encouraging a far more open and problem-solving approach to bullying and very effective where bullying is done within groups and is not too serious.

Perceptual Positions

Some schools are adopting a technique from NLP known as 'Perceptual Positions' as an effective tool within their overall bullying strategy. This is effective because:

1) It requires the child doing the bullying to examine what it may be like for the child being bullied.
2) The child being bullied gains greater insight to understand how they may appear to the other child as vulnerable to bullying.
3) Teachers and other staff can learn what it may be like to be in either parts of this interaction.
4) Everyone has more opportunity to learn empathy for others.

Using this requires careful supervision and words to maintain a safe environment for everyone concerned. However, the process does not require any spoken information, so children can feel safe in the process. This awareness can help to 'out' hidden problems and reduce incidents of bullying.

What are Perceptual Positions?

Me (1st) position is seeing, hearing and feeling the situation through your own eyes, ears, and emotions. You think in terms of what is important to you, and what you want to achieve.

The Other (2nd) position is stepping into the shoes of the other person and experiencing the situation as if you were them. When you are really in this position, then the way you (as the other person) are behaving makes sense. No matter how difficult or unreasonable someone's behaviour may seem, in their shoes it is normal and the best choice they have.

The Observer (3rd) position involves standing back from the situation and experiencing it as a detached observer. In your mind you are able to see and hear you and the other person as if you are a third person, or a fly on the wall.

We all naturally spend some time in each of the positions. Becoming habitually stuck in any of the positions has drawbacks.

Someone *stuck* in the **Self** position is likely to lack understanding and dismiss other people's feelings and ideas. They may push for the achievement of their own outcomes at the expense of others; as a result their achievements may be short lived, or backfire in some way. This may result in bullying behaviour.

Someone *stuck* in the **Other** position will identify with other people's needs and feelings at the expense of their own. This may stop themselves achieving, or thinking about what they really want because they constantly give others priority over themselves. This may make them reluctant to stand up for themselves.

Someone *stuck* in the **Observer** position will be a detached and unemotional observer of life. They are likely to be objective, analytical and lack involvement or commitment. This may inhibit engagement with situations 'in the moment'.

The ability to use all three positions in a balanced way leads to co-operative, assertive behaviour, and increases choice and understanding.

The procedure below may be used in many ways to improve understanding of the position of people other than ourselves. Individually, it may be used with:

- the child feeling bullied
- a parent or teacher of the child feeling bullied
- the child who is using bullying tactics

As a group exercise, it may be used with:

- a small group of children who observe bullying
- a group of teachers
- a family

However you use this approach in your own situation, the following instructions should be taken as a guide.

Using Perceptual Positions

Exploring a situation from the Self, Other, and Observer positions enables you to develop greater insight and understanding of the situation, and a more balanced and assertive approach in the future. Think of a situation, such as bullying, that you would like to be able to handle more resourcefully.

Stage 1
Go back to the situation. Step into the **Self** position.

Really see the **Other** person; her/his posture, gestures, body language etc.

Hear what you are saying and what the **Other** is saying, and what, if anything, you may be saying to yourself.

Notice what you feel being with the **Other** person.

Notice how long the situation is – run through it.

Stage 2*

Move to the **Other** person's position.

Step into the **Other's** shoes.

Really look at **Self** – (your) posture, gestures, body language etc. Hear what you (in **Other**) are saying and what **Self** is saying, and what if anything your internal voices are saying.

Notice what you feel as you stand alongside **Self**.

(*) If the explorer finds it difficult to step into the Other position invite them to stand just behind the person so that they can see/hear the situation without having to experience the feelings.

Stage 3

Step into the **Observer** position, like a fly on the wall, interested but detached from the situation.

Really see **Self** and **Other**; their posture, gestures, body language etc.

Hear what **Self** and **Other** are saying – notice the tones of voice, the words and the volumes.

What do you notice about **Self** and **Other**? Are there any patterns emerging, or patterns that are repeated from the past?

From the resourceful **Observer** position, how could you help **Self**? What insights and understanding could you offer that might change the way **Self** behaves and experiences the situation?

Stage 4

Step to **Self**, taking with you the insights from **Observer**.

Re-enact the situation with the new understanding.

Notice how it changes when you think and act differently.

Stage 5*

Step to **Other**.

Re-experience the situation.

Notice how the difference in the way **Self** is behaving changes the way you (as **Other**) experience the situation.

Stage 6

Step back to **Self**.

Notice how it is to be with **Other** with the understanding gained from previous step.

(*) If the explorer finds it difficult to step into the Other position invite them to stand just behind the person so that they can see/hear the situation without having to experience the feelings.

If facilitated safely and skilfully the benefits from the new learning can be immeasurable. Be confident!

Protecting yourself on the internet

The organisation 'Stopitnow!' (see page 55) suggests five SMART rules for keeping safe on the internet. The advice is about preventing child sexual abuse but the rules are entirely appropriate for preventing bullying on the internet as well.

SMART rules for staying safe on the internet

S – SAFE   Never give out personal information such as your name, address or phone number to people you don't know or don't trust.

M – MEETING   Never agree to meet anyone you don't know just because you have chatted on line.

A – ACCEPTING   Don't accept emails or open attachments from people you don't know or trust. Simply delete them or tell a parent.

R – RELIABLE   Don't trust everything someone says or tells you on the internet. They might be lying.

T – TELL   Tell your parents or a trusted adult if someone on line makes you feel uncomfortable or worried.

(adapted from 'stopitnow' pamphlet *The internet and children - what's the problem?*)

Useful books and resources

The *Being Yourself* catalogue (hand puppets and therapeutic games for professionals) can be obtained from Smallwood Publishing Ltd, The Old Bakery, Charlton House, Dour Street, Dover, Kent CT16 1ED
www.smallwood.co.uk

Bridge of Self-Confidence – a therapeutic and educational game for helping coping skills. Chesterfield: Winslow Press.
www.winslow-cat.com

Drost, J. (2004) *Bubblegum Guy: How to deal with how you feel.* Bristol: Lucky Duck Publishing.
www.luckyduck.co.uk

Hromek, R. (2004) *Game time: Games to promote social and emotional resilience for children aged 4 to 14.* Bristol: Lucky Duck Publishing Ltd
www.luckyduck.co.uk

Koeries, J., Marris, B. & Rae, T. (2005) *Problem Postcards: Social, Emotional and Behavioural Skills Training for Disaffected and Difficult Children aged 7 to 11.* Bristol: Lucky Duck Publishing.
www.luckyduck.co.uk

Mortimer, H. (2003) *Emotional Literacy and Mental Health in Early Years.* Stafford: QEd Publications.
www.qed.uk.com

Mortimer, H. (2006) *Behaviour Management in the Early Years.* Stafford: QEd Publications.
www.qed.uk.com

Mortimer, H. (2007) *Worry Box: Managing anxiety in young children.* Stafford: QEd Publications.
www.qed.uk.com

Mortimer, H. (2007) *Fireworks: Managing anger in young children.* Stafford: QEd Publications.
www.qed.uk.com

Mosley, J. (1998) *More Quality Circle Time.* Cambridge: LDA.
www.ldalearning.com

Plummer, D. (2007) *Helping Children to Build Self-Esteem: A Photocopiable Activities Book*. Chesterfield: Winslow Press.
www.winslow-cat.com

Rae, T. (2001) *Strictly Stress: Effective Stress Management: A Series of 12 Sessions for High School Students.* Bristol: Lucky Duck Publishing.
www.luckyduck.co.uk

Robinson, G. and Maines, B. (1997) *Crying for Help: The No Blame Approach to Bullying*. Bristol: Lucky Duck Publishing.
www.luckyduck.co.uk

Robinson, G. and Maines, B. (2003) *Safe to Tell: Producing an Effective Anti-bullying Policy in Schools*. Bristol: Lucky Duck Publishing.
www.luckyduck.co.uk

Sher, B. (1998) *Self-esteem Games: 300 Fun Activities That Make Children Feel Good About Themselves*. Chichester: John Wiley & Sons.
www.wiley.com

Shotton, G. (2002) *The Feelings Diary: Helping Pupils to Develop their Emotional Literacy Skills by Becoming More Aware of their Feelings on a Daily Basis*. Bristol: Lucky Duck Publishing.
www.luckyduck.co.uk

Stockton-on-Tees Educational Psychology Service (2001) *Managing your 4–8 year-old*. Stafford: QEd Publications.
www.qed.uk.com

Stockton-on-Tees Educational Psychology Service (2001) *Managing your 8–12 year-old*. Stafford: QEd Publications.
www.qed.uk.com

Stockton-on-Tees Educational Psychology Service (2002) *Managing your 13–16 year-old*. Stafford: QEd Publications.
www.qed.uk.com

Terry, R. and Churches, R. (2007) *NLP for Teachers: How to Be a Highly Effective Teacher*. Carmarthen: Crown House Publishing.
www.crownhouse.co.uk

Useful organisations

Anti-Bullying Alliance – an umbrella group of over 60 charitable and other organisations working in the anti-bullying field; has a range of information and resources for practitioners on their website.
www.anti-bullyingalliance.org.uk

Anti-Bullying Network – established at the University of Edinburgh to provide free anti-bullying support to school communities.
www.antibullying.net

Bullying UK – gives practical information and advice to young people and parents through their website and by email, includes work with schools, youth organisations, police forces and health trusts, running workshops.
email: help@bullying.co.uk
www.bullying.co.uk

Childline. Provides a 24 hour telephone helpline for children and young people.
Tel: 0800 1111
www.childline.org.uk

Parentline Plus – charity offering help and support through a range of free services by working for and with anyone who is parenting a child.
Tel: 0800 783 6783
www.parentlineplus.org.uk

Kidscape – national charity helping to prevent bullying and child abuse.
www.kidscape.org.uk

NLP Training – for information about individual or 'in house' training in Neuro-Linguistic Programming:
Train of Thought Training
34 Allerton Close, Northallerton DL7 8NX
Tel.01609 778543
enquire@trainofthought.org.uk
www.trainofthought.org.uk

NLP Practitioner & Behaviour Coach:
Jackie Johnson at Blue Roses, 34 Allerton Close, Northallerton DL7 8NX
Tel: 07988010519
jackie@blueroses.org.uk
www.blueroses.org.uk

Stop it now! – charity for protecting children from sexual abuse (looking into the problems caused by grooming and abuse on the internet).
www.stopitnow.org.uk

Winslow have a range of games and resources for working on many aspects of emotional intelligence, anger management, citizenship and social skills training.
www.winslow-cat.com